TEACHING IN A DIGITAL AGE

DR DHEERAJ MEHROTRA

Contents

Preface

Teaching in a Digital Age *is a priority toward excellence in Academics. The experience during the Pandemic proved to the masses that the technology used in digital learning could enable students to comprehend content matter more thoroughly and at a better preface to learning and doing. The students will become more involved in the learning process due to the variety of new instructional strategies teachers will be implementing in the classroom. Teaching in the digital preface doesn't only help you to identify your strengths and weaknesses; it enables your teachers to track your progress. They will have an easily accessible online record of all your work, and they'll be able to monitor your engagement. I am sure the book shall prove a significant share of the above.*

Happy Reading.

Cheers!

www.authordheerajmehrotra.com

CHAPTER ONE

Teaching Digitally- A Priority!

- *Teaching through technology must be a practise rather than an occasional occurrence if classrooms have to have a Wow feature.*

- *A quote by our Hon. Education Minister says,*

- *We need to restore the high respect and status of the profession to inspire and motivate our teachers. Our government is focusing on providing opportunities for self-improvement and continuous professional development. Not only in school education, but the faculty of our colleges and universities shall also learn about the latest technologies and innovations and different forms of pedagogies. We are building world-class centres for teacher training. The current budget has also made provisions for digital teachers with an allocation of ? six crores.*

- *The pandemic and unexpected geopolitical events have been unprecedented over the last two years. However, the positive part is that this challenging time has given birth to innovations. Several innovative models came up during the pandemic. Based on the principle that technology is an equaliser and enabler, the Union Budget made provisions for 200 new TV channels for education dissemination, allocating about ?930 crores in five years.*

- *Emergent technologies such as Artificial Intelligence, robotics and automation provide ample opportunities and challenges because scores of traditional jobs may fade away. But it will also bring roles more adapted to a new division of labour between humans, machines, and algorithms. Hence, the window of opportunity to reskill and upskill workers has become shorter, and one must act now to train the vast chunk of the youth.*

- *The 21st century is a century of knowledge. India, one of the oldest civilisations and knowledge societies, has a natural advantage in becoming a "captain" in navigating emerging economies toward a prosperous future.*

- *I believe after the Constitution, NEP 2020 is one document shaped after multiple levels of deliberations, discussions, and participatory dialogues across the country. Like the Constitution, NEP 2020 will lead us out of decades of dilemma and doubt and inculcate a deep-rooted pride in being Indian in thought, spirit, intellect, and deeds. It integrates students, teachers, parents, and society for holistic development and achieving their full human potential.*

- *Quote - Unquote!*

- *As teachers, we must not use technology as a silicon coating but harness the power of technology to connect with our students. No more, it is about copying and pasting, which we have done over the years. Power corrupts politicians, so PowerPoint corrupts the teachers if it has just slides and no explanations. For a matter of thought and intelligence, the platform should be shared for show rather than expecting it to be the only parcel for knowledge delivery. There is a specific need to implement a new way of teaching through technology; hence, digital pedagogy is required the most. The teachers need to introspect how children may learn in this networked environment. We can't simply take a textbook and deliver it digitally; instead, we need to explore the power to harness the best via connectivity and creativity to connect.*

- *We can't think and re-discover the chalk boy chalkboard. It is an intelligent board to deliver knowledge. What is required is a novel mindset of love, care and delivery of priorities for our children within classrooms. We ultimately need a different paradigm for teaching, a different pedagogy that talks about creation, control of chaos, connection to correcting, and consumption to creation. The teachers need to change their thinking about how they will use technology in education.*
-
-

There are reports, too, "Failed iPad Experiment Shows BYOD Belongs in Schools.", "LA. Cancels iPads-in-the-schools program: a failure of vision, not technology, despite our heavy investments in schools, loss of our strategy or the idea to implement the best technology in education. And above all, it seems to biseemsyailure of our pedagogy. One of our mistakes as educators is CTRL + C & CTRL + V. Necessarily as COPY and PASTE for this just can't solve the concerns but expands the issue in particular. This is one of the mistakes we get to govern while implementing technology in our schools.

- *Similarly, the conclusion fetches the scenario of apparent reasons for shifting teaching into a new realm. The core teaching principles having a shift need an activated model to conclude without looking back in perfection. The teachers need to be advocates for holistic education. This transforms the learners in a big way to assist learning and make it happen within the classrooms. Teachers need to keep things simple and do what works for them. For us, the teachers cannot teach the way we were taught. Above all, the students, at large, would only like the subject if they like the teacher, and this is one of the solitaire truths for any holy classroom in particular.*

Teachers need to have a wellness routine planning sheet, getting the win-win approach of the happiness index of the students, roll number wise. Indeed, classroom management has been identified as a primary concern for teachers. If they don't interact affectionately with the learners as bosses or clients, the class management appears slang. The teachers in the majority have a wrong notion that classroom management is much to do with discipline only and is limited to the children being quiet in the class.

In contrast, the goals include the identification of misconceptions about managing the teaching, the students and the consequences. The teachers of age need to broaden the very conception of classroom management and ultimately provide a framework among their colleagues for developing their classroom management plan. Engaging the children in instructions often leads to classroom management but is limited to a classic time only. A thoughtful physical environment for an activated classroom must be supported by establishing caring relationships and implementing engaging instructions.

- *The aid to learning concerning getting to know, learning to understand and executing for themselves became the new normal for months. The teachers also reflected with a view of identity, innovation and the reflective idea of making Teaching a Priority without the classrooms and the actual student in a room.*

- *Friends, post corona, we look forward to the new contributor to the stand-alone learning scenario. At taste, we tend to come together to the very reflective idea of making a difference in the classroom learning scenario now with the march of time and requirements.*

- *The pandemic truly brought us together not accurate but in the cloud with a fascinating learning opportunity, not by choice but by chance. This was not only limited to the educators, the teacher in particular, but also the parents and students. This positively came out in the preface towards the standardised reference for making learning a priority of the new age. With an attribute of facing the new normal, with reflective ideas, the narration, the identity on the go, fortunately, we could manage.*

- *For now, with the passing of time and orient modules, we are now recovering and revitalising the education platform. It is sure a brighter probability and, for that reason, a reality on standard regular times on cards. As we recall, we shifted to online teaching and learning, and now, when we are preparing to gain a step back physically in schools with so many doubts in everybody's minds, like, how to go? Ahead of all is the priority to task, is to Orient and make ware the people of the standards. And of the new normal, the teachers, the non-teaching staff and the parents. We also need to remember that it will not happen just by creating our tools for meetings. It's going to happen by reaching out to each stakeholder for assistance.*

- *The post-COVID arena demands, in particular, that's happening, and the schools need to be prepared for the new normal in a big way. The parents need to do what they never did, support the school management with the same approach of locating themselves as extended educators. Also, the schools need to harness and protect and conclude with the same idea of assuring the safety net.*

-

Above all, keeping the spectrum of COVID-19 also the objective shall be to promote the school-parents partnership, to enhance student safety measures. In addition, the other stakeholders need to consider this practice as a safety measure beyond the school campus. The reflective idea must be that we must contribute to and strengthen activity, the attributes schools need to follow, and environmental cleaning and decontamination procedures as a habit. Also, there has to be a reference routed to teachers via regular meetings every week to assure safety and regulations are followed in a big way.

•

As a priority, the schools must avoid any scheduled community events on school premises. The schools must also reinforce frequent hand washing and sanitisation and procure the necessary supplies. Also, as a priority, the schools need to update emergency plans and share the information via messages, videos and pictures. It is further mandatory on safety grounds that the schools be clean and explore information sharing needs as a favourable task towards the assurance of the health and the safety clause.

•

The modular execution needs concern, too, with all the students and the staff; in particular, the schools must ensure online communication channel is more robust and updated with the proper backup of data cloud and software update. Monitoring the school attendance and tracking the staff and students' participation is also essential. This takes the lead towards ensuring regular health updates in particular. Also, teachers must engage with updated and street-smart teaching strategies using various creative and innovative online and offline teaching platforms.

- *The teachers must engage the students with exercises and home study and promote podcasts as optional to Internet-based. In addition, the framework has to enable radio FM transmission for imparting lessons, and the coordinators, vice principals, and senior teachers need to unite to promote remote-based learning as a regular feature. Also, on the go is the priority with the significance of assuring the restroom signage posted detailing the Covid 19 recommendations. The students must be asked to practice these recommendations on a positive note and religiously.*

-

Everyday learning is obsolete in today's too fast-changing modern world.

- *In Digital learning, we get the materials instantaneously, and in everyday learning, we have to find out, which takes time.*

- *DL is more effective than everyday learning because it contains visuals, audio, and graphics to enhance learning power.*

- *Since digital learning is far more interactive and memorable than voluminous textbooks or one-sided lectures, they provide better context, a greater sense of perspective, and more engaging activities than traditional education methods. This allows students to better connect with the learning material.*

- *Easy to comprehend.*

- *Virtual visits possible*

- *Students understood the topic clearly, and they didn't forget easily.*

-

It has more impact than verbal explanation, restores more time, and involves all categories of learning skills.

- *As per NEP 2020, we have to introduce digital Learning in every class; it will increase students' confidence in implementing NEP 2020.*

- *increases access to education and knowledge while empowering students with a mindset and capabilities that set them up for success in their present and future*

- *DL helps students to acquire knowledge in less time.*

- *It enhances knowledge. Gives an idea about the subject.*

- *Provide better context, a greater sense of perspective, and more engaging activities than traditional education methods. Teaching can be made more effective and more efficient.*

•

Audio and visual-based education is more effective in everyday learning.

- *DIGITAL LEARNING GIVES PROPER EDUCATION BY EXPERTS IN PARTICULAR SUBJECTS. LEARNERS CAN TAKE MORE CONTENT USING ONLINE CONTENT COMPARED TO TRADITIONAL CLASSROOM LEARNING.*

- *Digital learning increases access to education and knowledge while empowering students with a mindset and capabilities that set them up for success in their present and future. DL allows students to learn at their own pace. And learners may get 3d experience in Science and Mathematics. Instead of imagining, visualisation helps them to understand in a better way.*

- *It gives more creativity and activity related wound RK; it activates the children. More learning with low time.*

- *DL provide better context, a greater sense of perspective, and more engaging activities than Normal learning.*

-

Active learning is enhanced in DL.

- *By helping children think outside their typical learning modes, digital learning inspires creativity and lets children feel a sense of accomplishment that encourages further education. Digital learning tools and technology fill the gaps where traditional classroom teaching falls behind.*

- *The long-lasting impact is there with an easy understanding.*

- *For more interactive and engaging activities.*

- *Digital learning uses videos which is not possible in everyday education.*

- *DL is far more interactive and memorable than voluminous textbooks or one-sided lectures. It provides better context, a great sense of perspective, and more engaging activities than traditional education methods.*

-

The learning via DL is Innovative, Clear, easily understandable and robust.

- *It empowers and gives confidence to the teachers while teaching. It is making the students also bright and develops effective seldirectiveve learning.*

- *Digital learning encompasses eLearning, continuous learning, blended learning and much more.*

- *It helps the students widen their knowledge and make learning enjoyable.*

- *Digital learning uses videos as an effective teaching method compared to Normal Learning; technology increases critical thinking skills, provides better context, an excellent mitre sense of perspective, and more engaging activities than traditional education methods.*

- *Everyday learning includes TLM like chalk, blackboard, etc., but digital learning platforms have tools like education robots, Wacklet, TeachingClass plus, etc.*

- *Provide better context, more engaging activities, and a greater perspective.*

- *Since the world around us has this technology, we should also adapt and update along with this.*

- *Digital learning empowers their efficiency and productivity. Also, digital learning tools and technology increases critical thinking skills, which are the basis for the growth of reasoning skill. Students also develop positive feelings and the confidence to learn new things,*

- *Digital learning increases access to education and knowledge while empowering students with a mindset and capabilities that set them up for success in their present and future. Students can learn through their own devices at any time and anywhere.*

- *Digital learning is more interactive and memorable than voluminous textbooks. They provide better context, a greater sense of perspective, and more engaging activities than traditional education methods.*

- *We develop learners' attitudes towards learning, which helps overcome potential challenges. It is essential in Maths gives visualise the concepts.*

- *More effective, more practical, and easily understandable is very important for each student.*

- *Digital learning increases access to education and knowledge while empowering students with a mindset and capabilities that set them up for success in their present and future.*

- *Digital learning increases access to education and knowledge while empowering students with a mindset and capabilities that set them up for success in their present and future.*

- *Learners can take more content using online content. Digital learning makes the students' work more accessible. Online schooling has been an important tool to sustain skills development during school closures, considering the alternative of no schooling. There are still concerns that online learning may have been a sub-optimal substitute for face-to-face instruction, especially in the absence of universal access to infrastructure (hardware and software) and inadequate preparation among teachers and students for the unique demands of online teaching-learning pose.*

- *It creates interest in students and is beneficial to understanding the concepts quickly.*

- *Digital learning is also essential as, during the pandemic, the education of the students could be taken care of by taking online classes. We all know how well versed the students are with the latest technology and different learning apps, and they tend to learn things quickly digitally.*

- *It helps to make the concept clear to students. More advanced, more technical, practical and demand time. It is straightforward to understand, Motivates everyone during the teaching process. The students can learn fastest through digital learning.*

-

To show the internal parts easily in the classroom. Digital Learning is visual and audio-based, so education is more effective.

- *It's useful for better understanding a topic using audio and video clip and links to the students.*

- *It is undoubtedly Effective, Practical, innovative, impressive and easily understandable.*

- *It enhances everyday learning and promotes the use of current technologies to the newer generation. We can also teach them practical and constructive internet and technology use.*

- *DL makes learning more accessible and more effective. It makes it easy to understand the concept.*

- *Students can enhance their thinking and working capabilities with the use of IT. They grow from introverts to extroverts.*

-

To understand the students‘ behaviours and communicate with the students more effectively.

- *Learning can be done from the place, but it can be connected with anybody worldwide—lots of benefits.*

- *It makes the class more interactive and exciting and helps memorise things quickly.*

- *DL taught us to be updated in this technological era. Silence can be effective—organised classroom control.*

- *Digital tools and platforms are becoming integral to our personal and working lives. Digital learning increases access to education and knowledge while empowering students with a mindset and capabilities that set them up for success in their present and future.*

- *Digital learning is essential to common understanding because DL increases access to education and knowledge while empowering students with a mindset and capabilities that set them up for success in their present and future.*

- *It's a good learning platform.*

- *DL help easy explain through children can understand easily.*

- *Digital learning increases access to education and knowledge while empowering students with a mindset and capabilities that set them up for success in their present and future.*

- *The digital learning system enables students to analyse what they need to know to search and use online resources.*

- *Digital learning increases access to education and knowledge while empowering students with a mindset and capabilities that set them up for success in their present and future, whereas everyday learning is also effective.*

- *Provide better context, an excellent mitre sense of perspective, and more engaging activities than traditional education methods.*

- *It provides a good platform for learning inside or outside the classroom.*

- *.Digital learning can be accessed anywhere in the world.*

- *It's a natural and solid connection to the subject of children.*

- *DL empowers their efficiency and productivity.*

- *Digital learning grasps students' attention and teaches all topics in detail. It helps them learn enthusiastically.*

- *Since digital learning is far more interactive and memorable than voluminous textbooks or one-sided lectures, they provide better context, a greater sense of perspective, and more engaging activities than traditional education methods. This allows students to better connect with the learning material.*

-

We can teach online, saving time, meetings, and more clarity by sharing PDFs or videos.

- *Digital learning is any instructional practice that ultimately helps students.*

- *DL increases access to education and knowledge, provides transparency into the learning process, and enhances the learning experience.*

- *The importance of DL over everyday learning makes the classroom joyful.*

- *Digital tools and platforms are becoming integral to our personal and working lives. Digital learning increases access to education and knowledge while empowering students with a mindset and capabilities that set them up for success in their present and future.*

- *It promotes learning technology.*

- *-Helps in understanding quickly.*

-

- Does not force a person into one sitting.

- *Digital tools and platforms are becoming integral to our personal and working lives. Digital learning increases access to education and knowledge while empowering students with a mindset and capabilities that set them up for success in their present and future. Plenty of data suggests that simply giving learners access to devices doesn't necessarily lead to better outcomes; thoughtful integration and actively adopting a digital mindset are needed for digital learning to enhance the overall student experience.*

- *DL is more effective than everyday learning because our mindset catches early audio-visual images. It can present the needed information very shortly quickly.*

- *It generates the learner's interest as graphical software significantly affects the learner's mind comparedeverydayrmal learning. Learning becomes more fun and engaging. It is an interactive session. During the hard time of the pandemic, we continued the teaching-learning process without a break just because of digital tools.*

- *It's more versatile and engaging in a different environment and challenging times.*

- *They provide a greater sense of perspective and more engaging activities.*

- *1. It makes teaching more effective.*

- *2. It makes individual teaching.*

- *3. It is very effective even during pandemics.*

- *We may teach from home using technology—Time-saving, practice, and sharing subject materials digitally.*

- *Digital Learning can enhance learning experiences, save teachers time, enable teachers to better tailor learning to student needs, track student progress, provide transparency into the learning process for all stakeholders, and much more.*

-

DL learning is a based method of learning.

- *Deep learning is part of a broader family of machine learning methods based on artificial neural networks with representation learning.*

- *Since digital learning is far more interactive and memorable than voluminous textbooks or one-sided lectures, they provide better context, a greater sense of perspective, and more engaging activities than traditional education methods. This allows students to better connect with the learning material.*

- *It makes the teaching effective and creative, helps them, and exposes them beyond the books.*

- *It will create interest among students and help learners understand the content well. The usage of technology makes the class more interesting.*

- *Digital learning increases access to education and knowledge while empowering students with a mindset and capabilities that set them up for success in their present and future.*

- *Since digital learning is far more interactive and memorable than voluminous textbooks or one-sided lectures, they provide better context, a greater sense of perspective, and more engaging activities than traditional education methods. This allows students to better connect with the learning material.*

- *It is to understand the concept.*

- *Learning by using visual online resources for better understanding*

- *Very important for online digital learning management*

- *It is an essential addition to the learning experience.*

- *Deep learning is a deep neural network consisting of many different layers, and each layer comprises many other nodes.*

-

Deep learning is a deep neural network consisting of many different layers, and each layer comprises many other nodes.

- *Digital learning provides better context, a greater sense of perspective, and more engaging activities than traditional education methods.*

- *It's personalised learning having engaging lessons with flexibility and roe clock resou*

- *Digital learning is far more interactive and memorable than voluminous textbooks or one-sided lectures; they provide better context, a greater sense of perspective, and more engaging activities than traditional education methods. This allows students to better connect with the learning material.*

- *A significant learning rate allows the model to learn faster at the cost of arriving at the suboptimal final set of weights.*

- *Digital learning helps students to see and learn. It provides broader learning materials and opportunities. Elements of digital learning are easy to access, and watching animation and pictures enhance the learning process. It is also a great teaching aid for the teachers.*

- *Everyday teaching may not be practical, whereas DL can increase our teaching abilities.*

- *Enable the student's experience through cognitive and pervasive connectivity*

- *Interactive, student-centric*

- *Digital tools and platforms are becoming integral to our personal and working lives. Digital learning increases access to education and knowledge while empowering students with a mindset and capabilities that set them up for success in their present and future.*

- *Machine learning requires less computing power; deep understanding typically needs less ongoing human intervention.*

- *It is more attractive and exciting, and students retain it for a more extended period.*

- *DL accessible anytime, anywhere, by any means*

- *This could entail using sites, services, programs, teaching tools, and technologies like study aids built for at-home use. Even social networks and communications platforms can be used to create and manage digital assignments and agendas. It empowers students by making them more interested in learning and expanding their horizons. DL increases their efficiency and productivity. In addition to engaging students, digital learning tools and technology sharpen critical thinking skills, the basis for developing analytic reasoning.*

- *Digital learning increases access to education and knowledge while empowering students with a mindset and capabilities that set them up for success in their present and future.*

-

Through DL, We can share a lot of information, i.e. from all over the world, with our students using different digital learning tools.

- *It Saves time, is easily accessible, competition is more minor, and better retention.*

- *DL increases access to education and knowledge while empowering students with a mindset and capabilities that set them up for success in their present and future.*

- *Students don't need to schedule much time to acquire the new courses. They can learn through their own devices at any time and anywhere. Moreover, traditional learning has become expensive, whereas E-Learning is cheaper than the former.*

- *Learning tools and technology enable students to develop practical self-directed learning skills.*

-

The learning process becomes easy and smooth; students can be engaged with a new idea and digital equipment.

- *It is handy, beneficial and quick, and effective.*

- *increases access to education and knowledge while empowering students with a mindset and capabilities that set them*

- *Digital learning is the learning in which the students watch and listen. So the impact is more as compared to everyday learning.*

- *More attractive ways of learning*

- *Very Effective.*

- *Online learning is more effective than traditional learning because it gives you time and freedom. One can open study videos on their own time—no need to go to an institution to attend lectures.*

-

it makes the student's work easier it increases knowledge

- *It helps to recapitulate the previous things.*

- *Grasps the subject well into the students*

- *It is more interactive. They provide better context and more engaging activities than everyday learning.*

- *Many platforms for the same subject.Many more different ideas about the subject matter. We are sharing views through various social media.*

- *It makes learning enjoyable, joyful, and logical thinking.*

- *We can learn and demonstrate many things related to our subject using DL.*

- *Both have equal importance, but a situation like covid 19 DL has the edge over everyday learning.*

- *Topics should be understood easily.*
- *Digital learning provides more variety to learn at a single time. It gives more clarity to the students.*
- *Digital learning enhances student accountability, improves learning experiences, provides transparency into the learning process., and increases access to education and knowledge.*
- *It gives more information to the students to gain more knowledge about their schoworkrks.*
- *Ideal and very enhancement of knowledge*
- *Students can get a wide range of accessibility for their learning materials...*
- *They become highly technically developed.*
- *Digital learning empowers their efficiency and productivity. Also, digital learning tools*

and technology increases critical thinking skills, which are the basis for the growth of reasoning skill.

- *Increases access to education and knowledge.*

- *Empowers with a mindset and capabilities that set up for success.*

- *Digital learning makes class exciting and engaging. Assessment becomes more accessible as it reduces the load of corrections.*

- *It helps to learn quickly, interestingly. Enhance learning and make teaching enjoyable.*

- *Digital learning increases access to education and knowledge while empowering the students with a mindset and capabilities that set them up for success in their present and future. It can be more effective if a child pays attention .with the help of videos, games, quizzes, and other related subjects, the content lesson can be exciting and easy.*

- *Digital tools and platforms are becoming integral to our personal and working lives. Digital learning increases access to education and knowledge while empowering students with a mindset and capabilities that set them up for success in their present and future. Digital learning makes education available at all times, not only during the 8 hours students spend in school. Now they can learn whenever they want. As we know, every child has their own pace of learning; now, they can learn at their speed, which will help them understand the concepts better and in-depth.*

- *It is easy to use and store for the future, and it also helps to give references and examples. Digital learning makes the students learn easier. It gives students more information to gain knowledge about their school work.*

- *Digital tools and platforms are becoming integral to our personal and working lives. Digital learning provides access to education and knowledge while empowering students with a mindset and capabilities that set them up for success in their present and future.*

-

Digital tools and platforms are becoming integral to our personal and working lives. Digital learning increases access to education and knowledge while empowering students with a mindset and capabilities that set them up for success in their present and future. Digital learning is a more practical education because oral is not effective as visual.

- *It is essential to make a poster for online classes, better performance and technical knowledge in the present scenario. Course materials are created, shared with others, and developed together in the cloud in the digital era. With digital instruction, students learn to accept greater personal responsibility early while improving communication and teamwork.*

- *Digital learning increases access to education and knowledge while empowering students with a mindset and capabilities that set them up for success in their present and future.*

- *DL has far more reach than everyday learning and has a more significant impact on students.*

- *A library containing code and data can be used by multiple programs simultaneously.*

- *Digital learning enables students to analyse what they need to know to search and use online resources.*

- *For sure, it is so straightforward to implement.*

- *It helps teaching-learning be more effective and exciting, making concepts more transparent and innovative.*

- *It is as important as our new lifestyle.*

- *It is easier to understand,d students can know without any hesitation.*

- *Digital learning increases access to education and knowledge while empowering students with a mindset and capabilities that set them up for success in their present and future.*

-

Online education enables the teacher and the student to set their own learning pace, and there's the added flexibility of setting a schedule that fits everyone's agenda. As a result, using an online educational platform allows for a better balance of work and studies, so there's no need to give anything up.

- *Machine learning requires less computing power; deep understanding typically needs less ongoing human intervention.*
- *It is more effective than Normal learning.*
- *To make the weak and less interested students indulge in the subjects, bond them with the different topics.*
- *This is effective teaching.*
- *..Enhance experiential learning*
- *Digital learning empowers their efficiency and productivity, and digital learning tools and technology increase critical thinking skills, which are the basis for the growth of*

Reasoning skills. As a result, the students also developed Positive feelings and confidence to learn new things.

- *Digital learning increases access to education & knowledge while empowering students with a mindset & capabilities that set them up for success in future and present.*

- *Digital learning empowers their efficiency and productivity. Also, digital learning tools and technology increase critical thinking skills, which are the basis for the growth of reasoning skills.*

- *Digital learning provides more engaging activities than traditional methods. It can enhance learning experiences, track student progress and save teachers time. Overall it enables teachers to cater to the needs of different children.*

- *Learning tools and technology enable students to develop practical self-directed learning skills.*

-

Students using digital learning tools and technology become more engaged in the process and more interested in growing their knowledge base; they may not even realise that they're actively learning since they're learning through engaging methods such as peer education, teamwork, problem-solving, reverse teaching, concept maps, gamification, staging, role-playing, and storytelling.

- *All information is ready when used in classroom teaching, improving worldwide education knowledge.*

- *Digital learning provides voluminous teaching content rather than textbook teaching.*

- *Digital learning can be accessed from any location.*

- *Digital learning is essential and essential for average knowledge in any subject. We use that digital learning for teaching,*

- *DL is necessary as we can learn while not presenting physically in the school or training institute.*

- *Videos and other digital projects are very readily available for DL.*
- *It develops psychomotor skills.*
- *Indeed, students get better exposure while following digital learning.*
- *Which helps them in their later life.*
- *Its a learning transformation and create an engaging learning experience for the students over Normal Learning*
- *Digital learning increases access to education and knowledge for every student.*
- *Interactive and student-centric*
- *Feature generation automation*
-

Digital learning is the best way of teaching in which we can use various tools to make the topic accessible and understandable compared to everyday learning. We can also reach the child if he cannot regularly attend school as we have done in pandemics.

- *Dl is handy and beneficial over Normal learning.*

- *Great sense of perspective and more engaging activities.*

- *Creates curiosity & interest among students to learn. It makes teaching effective.*

- *Education by doing.*

- *Students will simply get more exposure to complicated concepts through videos and pictures. Using digital learning tools, teachers can provide audio-visual and interactive experiences to the students.*

- *Deep learning is a part of a broader family of machine learning methods based on artificial neural networks with representation learning.*

- *DL increases access to education and knowledge while empowering students with a mindset and capabilities that set them up for success in their present and future.*

- *When we learn digital learning, we become familiar with the technology, which can not be helpful with everyday knowledge.*

- *Easily access... Very simple and easy to learn.*

- *It is more interesting than everyday learning.*

- *Digital learning Makes the class interesting; students understand better the concept through PPT, video, games, quizzes etc.*

- *This is excellent learning at home.*

- *Digital learning tools and platforms are integral to our personal and working lives. Digital learning increases access to education and knowledge while empowering students with capabilities that set them up for success in their present and future.*

- *Increases critical thinking and reasoning in students. It makes students enthusiastic about learning as well.*

- *It's exciting and valuable for new studies.*

- *The content can be presented flexibly and supported with visuals.*

- *Makes students smarter*

- *Helpful in teaching*

- *Digital learning increases access to education and knowledge while empowering students with a mindset and capabilities that set them up for success in their present and future.*

- *Through DL, concepts will be more apparent to the students than in everyday learning.*

-

Improves children's efficiency and productivity.

•

It's too influential in the teaching-learning process.

•

DL will help make students more creative and help them explore more and more, as we all know that a book may have limitations. But using various online tools, we can help students understand the concepts of any given topic very quickly. Using online tools or cloud storage, we will allow a child to get connected to the topics and chapters, and by that, we can help them grow up and be associated with the advanced technology. AI and robotics will allow us to let clear our doubts.

•

Digital learning increases access to education and knowledge while empowering students with a mindset and capabilities that set them up for success in their present and future.

•

Digital learning management helps the learning culture in schools at its priority.

•

Since digital learning is far more interactive and memorable than voluminous textbooks or one-sided lectures, they provide better context, a greater sense of perspective, and more engaging activities than traditional education methods. This allows students to better connect with the learning material.

•

Digital learning and instructional practice ultimately help students; it's helpful for students to get online education.

•

Digital tools and platforms are becoming integral to our personal and working lives. Digital learning increases access to education and knowledge while empowering students with capabilities that set them for sector success in their present and future.

•

Digital learning makes us teach innovatively. It saves time, and we can explore many things while teaching, such as presentations, postures, lab,s animations etc. I have learnt the importance of learning and teaching through some websites Mindoro. Com, teacher tube. Com. Wallet. Com etc. Throughout session was excellent. It was very informative. Thank you.

•

DL has proven to be more effective with the students as it is more exciting, and the students are more attentive and more interactive in the classrooms as they understand better with the help of visual aids.

- *Students become Smarter: Students develop practical self-directed learning skills when exposed to new learning tools and technology.*

- *Since the world around us has this technology, we should also adapt and update along with this.*

- *Digital Learning has become a critical learning method for today's generation as children can gain new and updated information on any topic they want. I wouldn't say that everyday learning is terrible. Still, for the current generation, DL has become the go-to, as there are a lot of innovations and exciting methodologies which can make even slow learners grow at a tremendous rate. For the gifted, DL has broadened the area of critical thinking.*

•

Digital Learning increases access to education and knowledge while empowering students with a mindset and capabilities that set them up for success in their present and future.

- *Digital learning increases access to education and knowledge while empowering students with a mindset and capabilities that set them up for success in their present and future.*

- *It gives control over time, place etc.*

- *Digital learning is beneficial instead of chalk and talk.*

- *.More engaging*

- *You can learn from anywhere.*

- *It plays a vital role in improving critical thinking and reasoning skills.*

- *Students improved their computer skills.*

- *Learning quickly & time needed digital learning.*
- *.Visualisation increased by students.*
- *It provides us with technological knowledge.*
- *It makes us aware of technological tools.*
- *This makes the teaching easy to learn and remember for a longer time.*
- *.DL is more interactive and engaging than Normal Learning. It generates interest in learning in students and inspires creativity. As information can be shared rapidly, it boosts learning. The retention power of a concept also increases. It makes learning enjoyable.*
- *Classes become attractive and interactive.*
- *Digital learning is replacing traditional educational methods more and more each day. Digital learning makes students*

smarter. DL is making students self-motivated. DL is rapidly increasing information sharing.

- *Provides better context, and more engaging activities*

- *It will make the classroom more alive and active.*

- *It makes education more productive by closing learning gaps and accelerating progress.*

- *Interactive, memorable, more engaging, more activities can e included.*

- *Another term used for distance education is planned to teach and learning experience conducted using various technologies on-ground and electronically at remote sites.*

- *It is essential.*

- *It encompasses applying a broad spectrum of practices, including blended and virtual learning.*

- *Digital learning is better than everyday learning.*

- *It gets knowledge and is easy to get.*

- *A greater sense of perspective and more engaging activities than the traditional education method.*

- *Digital Learning is far more interactive and memorable than voluminous textbooks or one-sided lectures; they provide better context, a greater sense of perspective, and more engaging activities than traditional education methods. This allows students to better connect with the learning material. It enables teachers to better tailor learning to students‘ needs, tracks students’ progress and provides transparency into the learning process.*

- *LongerMore prolonged impact, interactive, and make participants get involved.*

-

To create practice-oriented learning.

- *Digital learning increases access to education and knowledge by empowering students.*

- *I can improve better.*

- *Digital learning provides better context, a greater sense of perspective, and more engaging activities than traditional education methods.*

- *It is more interactive and memorable.*

- *The way of teaching and advanced learning.*

- *It varies very important to students and teachers. Because due to progress in teaching methods.*

- *Deep learning is a deep neural network comprised of many different layers, and each layer consists of many other nodes.*

-

Since digital learning is far more interactive and memorable than voluminous textbooks or one-sided lectures, they provide better context, a greater sense of perspective, and more engaging activities than traditional education methods. This allows students to better connect with the learning material.

- *Increases access to education and knowledge while empowering students with a mindset and capabilities that set them up for success in their present and future.*

- *Digital tools and platforms are becoming integral to our personal and working lives. Digital learning increases access to education and knowledge while empowering students with a mindset and capabilities that set them up for success in their present and future.*

- *DL is far more interactive and memorable than the big textbooks or one-sided lectures; they provide better context, a greater sense of perspective, and more engaging activities than traditional educational methods. This allows students to connect with the learning materials.*

-

Provide better content, a greater sense of perspective, and more engaging activities than traditional educational methods. This allows students to better connect with learning material. Far more interactive & memorable than textbooks. It makes students concentrate on the subject rather than be distracted by voluminous books.

- *DL increases access to education and knowledge while empowering students with a mindset for success.*

- *Digital learning makes learning more practical and easy to grasp than everyday learning.*

- *Improve teacher's support, prepare students for the futuImproveeoves attentively-guided learning.*

- *As really very effective for the conceptual clarity of the students.*

- *Digital learning increases access to education and knowledge while empowering students with a mindset and capabilities that set them up for success in their present and future.*

- *Digital learning increases access to education and knowledge while empowering students with a mindset and capabilities that set them up for success in their present and future.*

- *It is beneficial as per the current scenario to have blended learning. DL helps to understand students‘ behaviour and needs. It has more effective communication with introverted students and provides personalised guidance to the students.*

- *Provide better content, a greater sense of perspective, and more engaging activities than traditional educational methods. This allows students to better connect with learning material. Far more interactive & memorable than textbooks. It makes students concentrate on the subject rather than be distracted by voluminous books.*

- *A library containing code and data can be used by multiple programs simultaneously.*

-

It gives a proper explanation visually with the help of graphics, which help understand better.

- *The learners can take more content using digital learning compared to everyday learning. Digital learning enhances learning experiences and enables teachers to modify their teaching based on student needs. Also, Digital learning increases access to education and empowers students.*

- *DL is best for the student. Here, students can use both audio-visual systems for learning, which helps them rove their skills.*

- *Digital learning increases access to education and knowledge while empowering students with a mindset and capabilities that set them up for success in their present and future.*

- *Digital learning increases access to education and knowledge while empowering students with a mindset and capabilities that set them up for success in their present and future.*

-

Digital learning is making students self-motivated and more accountable.

- *Increasing is increasing students' employability with Digital Learning Tools and Technology.*

- *It enhances your critical thinking.*

- *DL is more students centred and attracts the attention of learners.*

- *The most important benefit of digital learning is the opportunity to help every student learn at the best pace and path for them.*

- *The most important benefit of digital learning is the opportunity to help every student learn at the best pace and path for them.*

- *Digital Learning elevates teaching and learning. Community brings technology and pedagogy closer together. A curriculum-aligned teaching and learning platform with interactive textbooks anand analytical and assessment support- easy to use and all in one place.*

- *It teaches the students to be more responsible, conna its students to the real world, and prepares them for the workforce.*

- *It acts as a booster dose.*

- *More practical output, less time consuming, more production and impressive. The Learner can take more content than everyday learning; It empowers students by getting them to be more interested in learning and expanding their horizons.*

- *Digital learning increases access to education and knowledge while empowering students with a mindset and capabilities that set them up for success in their present and future.*

- *DIGITAL LEARNING ENABLES LEARNERS TO PUT TO DESIGN THE IDEAS THAT CROP IN THEIR MINDS. VISUALISATION OF CONCEPTS THROUGH DIGITAL 3-D MODELS IS MUCH EASIER AS COMPARED TO THE*

USUAL 1 OR 2-D TEXTBOOK METHOD.

- *Digital learning is replacing everydaeducationng more and more each day. DL makes students smarter as they learn new tools in technology, learning skills, online resources, etc. These sharpen critical thinking skills, the basis for developing analytical reasoning. Children who explore open-ended questions with imagination and logic learn how to make decisions instead of temporarily memorising the textbook.*

- *It empowers students by getting them more interested in learning and expanding their horizons.*

- *Digital learning allows students to better connect with learning material.*

- *..It is more effective, less time-consuming, exciting and more output-oriented.*

-

Digital learning increases access to education and knowledge while empowering students with a mindset and capabilities that set them up for success in their present and future.

- *Digital learning increases access to education and knowledge, while Normal learning is the process of mainly learning with average or above-average quality.*

- *Digital Learning provides increased access to knowledge and improves critical thinking and reasoning skills in an environment friendly to learners, saving both time and money with interactive content as per personalised learning.*

- *It enhances logical and critical thinking and makes learning exciting and joyful.*

- *It is more helpful for the students as it is crucial to make learning comfortable.*

- *Artificial Intelligence is the concept of creating smart, innovative, intelligent machines. Machine Learning is a subset of artificial intelligence that helps you build AI-*

driven applications. Deep Learning is a subset of machine learning that uses vast data and complex algorithms to train a model.

- *Digital learning adds the 'wow element to the learning process. It's an excellent aid for visual and audio learners. It makes the learning process exciting and enjoyable.*

- *It helps to explore a new topic, and it is vast.*

- *Digital learning increases access to education and knowledge while empowering students with a mindset and capabilities that set them up for success in their present and future.*

- *A good solution for every question*

- *Digital Learning is fast, complete and modern.*

- *There are plenty of benefits of digital learning in transforming a child's life, like motor skills, decision making, cultural awareness, and improved academic performance. it has content variety, highly interactive*

- *Provide better context, an excellent mitre sense of perspective, and more engaging activities than traditional education methods.*

- *More attractive than ever.*

- *To achieve one's goals effectively and efficiently.*

CHAPTER TWO

The Delightful Coding

CODING, CODING, CODING!!!

To my surprise....... Friends.

Over the year, Yes, just over the year, we have heard the term CODING by vendors of repute marching in the business arena to club the learning with commercial takeaways. How do I think that a 12-year-old with a two-week coding course can earn millions in the wildest of my dreams? It is kidding, and so it is!!

Friends, as a computer science author and a teacher myself, I believe it is just like minting money which the schools could not, but the private vendors did over time, keeping the pace to the spectrum of CORONA as an excuse.

According to the ***NEP****, classes on* ***coding*** *will be initiated for students from class 6 onwards. Please get to know about how it is different from Computer Programming.*

As per McKinsey Global Institute, from 2020 onwards, 90%+ of all jobs will require significantly more creativity. We as Educators need to help unleash our child's imagination and enable a mindset shift from being consumers of technology to its creators.

Let us Embark our children on a coding adventure!

Coding certainly helps kids develop problem-solving skills such as perseverance, trial and error, and understanding cause and effect. They use analytical thinking and reasoning skills and math and literacy skills. Coding challenges children to think creatively and pursue innovative solutions. The narration has to be equipped with the landmark success we have had in our schools with the introduction of computer science as a stand-alone subject.

Here coding is just an add-on to its fertility with Robotics/ Artificial Intelligence/ Computer Programming. Some of the fascinating aspects relate to a child's improvement in reasoning, problem-solving, and ability to abstract concepts.

The march is with the inception of another term for computer programming as a process via decision making, data structures, classes and objects, to count a few. The integration is marched with the upgraded design thinking framework and artificial intelligence format. The topics the teachers may cover under the so-called CODING as a tag may include creating a game, which increases thinking skills by 60%, enhances problem-solving and boosts creativity and computational thinking skills.

The objective is toward computer programming via:

- *Connect*
- *Concept*
- *Code*
- *Contemplate*
- *Continue*

The 5 C Learning framework activates learning by doing as one of the lively examples of Experiential learning in particular. Some of the defined and desired languages we as computer teachers reflect on teaching via CODING include JAVA, C++ and Python.

We also aim to teach design, making and coding circuits with safety measures to create IoT projects of intelligent homes, offices, Industries and smart cities in a stimulating environment. The coding language, like Python, also helps develop AI to collect, process and store high-quality data in files and databases for analytics and visualisations and create A.I. powered games, chatbots, prediction and forecasting tools with deep UI/ UX Interface in particular.

How to Learn Coding?

As an Educator and a UDEMY Instructor, I believe it is perfectly OK to start learning to code using free resources. One can figure out free online courses and tutorials to learn a few basics.

At what age to start coding?

Well, there is no right age to code or learn to code. With the advancement in the Tech Age, it is always good to start in prior years to get an edge over others. Early exposure for age five and above is recommended as the children have an excellent grasping power at that level.

Some Smart Platforms to Learn Coding

Include, Codecademy, one of the biggest and most beginner-friendly coding platforms worldwide. FreeCodeCamp is another popular platform for learning, among others.

This is just another list and reference for the needful. It is worth mentioning a list for the benefit of our educators on the go:

Useful Websites for coding:

1. www.codecademy.com

2. www.lynda.com

3. www.udemy.com

4. www.udacity.com

5. www.coursera.org

6. *www.w3schools.com*

7. *www.thenewboston.org*

8. *www.programmr.com*

9. *www.codeavengers.com*

10. *www.codeschool.com*

11. *www.learnstreet.com*

12. *www.teamtreehouse.com*

13. *www.sqlzoo.net*

14. *www.codehs.com*

15. *www.teamtreehouse.com*

16. *www.html5rocks.com*

17. *www.codepen.io*

18. *www.sitepoint.com*

19. *www.tutorialspoint.com*

20. *www.javatpoint.com*

21. *www.cplusplus.com*

22. *www.learncpp.com*

23. *www.tutorialspoint.com*

24. *www.cprogramming.com*

25. *www.stackoverflow.com*

26. *www.learncodethehardway.org*

27. *www.bloc.io*

28. *www.howtocode.io*

29. *www.edx.org*

30. *www.instructables.com*

31. *www.developer.apple.com*

32. *www.developer.android.com*

33. *www.developers.google.com*

34. *www.developer.mozilla.org*

35. *www.msdn.microsoft.com*

36. *www.dev.opera.com*

37. *www.www.developphp.com*

38. *www.quackit.com*

39. *www.htmlite.com*

40. *www.siteduzero.com*

41. *www.dreamincode.net*

42. *www.phpbuddy.com*

43. *www.php.net*

44. *www.microsoftvirtualacademy.com*

45. *www.professormesser.com.*

Some of the marginal inclusion in the course for coding may include Arduino, Scratch, Python, 3D Design, MIT APP Inventor, Circuit Simulation and Web Designing.

App Geyser helps develop Apps at a level of essential learning and execution.

Here I would like to recommend a special mention of:

Source: Credits www.authordheerajmehrotra.com

9 798887 496252

Printed by Libri Plureos GmbH in Hamburg, Germany